Written by Catherine Zoller

Pictures by Mr. Sketches

"GETTING THESE BOOKS IN PEOPLE'S HANDS SO PEOPLE'S HANDS PICK UP THE BOOK."

ABOUT THE AUTHOR

Catherine Zoller is a writer who lives in Tulsa, Oklahoma,
With a husband, three kids and half a college diploma.

Many years ago the Lord spoke to her one night
And said simply and clearly, "I want you to write."

So she jumped out of bed and grabbed paper and pen
And waited on the sofa for Him to speak to her again.

At last came the dawn with the dew and the mist,
But all she had written was half a grocery list.

Still she never forgot the words spoken that night;
All she had to learn was that His timing's always right.

Now she's written some rhymes that tell the Bible story
From Genesis to Revelation which reveal God's glory.

The hope in her heart is to show everyone
That reading God's Word can be lots of fun.

It will instruct you and teach you and change your heart,
And this little book is designed to help you start!

Matthew: The Rhyme and Reason Series by Catherine Zoller
Copyright ©2010 by Catherine Zoller

ISBN 978158169-3430
For worldwide distribution

Evergreen Press • P.O. Box 191540 • Mobile AL 36619 • 800-367-8203
You can learn more about Catherine Zoller at www.catherinezoller.com.

ABOUT THE ILLUSTRATOR

Artist Mr. Sketches is also known by some
As Mr. David Wilson, and he thinks art is fun.

The nickname Mr. Sketches came from a T.V. show
That TBN broadcast for three years in a row.

His lovely wife, Karen, likes to teach the first grade;
They moved around a bit, but when they got to Tulsa stayed.

Art from the heart helps God's kids succeed
So as David sketches, this is his creed:

"Whatever Reason or Rhyme, whatever season or time,
With a broad point or with fine, it's time to draw the line!"

DEDICATION

This book is dedicated to the most patient man I know,
Who believed in this series all those many years ago.

His persistence and kindness never once swayed,
And the help and encouragement can never be repaid.

From the moment he saw it, he knew it could grow;
And he saw great potential when the others said no.

His name is Keith Carroll, and he's an awesome guy
To whom I'll be forever grateful, even after I die!

3

The gospel of Matthew was written by a man.
It came from the Holy Spirit through this apostle's hand.

Matt was hated by other Jews because he collected the tax
That was demanded by the Romans then filled his own sacks.

A tax collector was usually a traitor and a thief,
'Cause they made themselves rich and caused others grief.

But Jesus came to Matthew because He saw inside his heart;
He loved him and changed him and gave him a fresh start.

Matt was one of the twelve apostles who were by Jesus' side,
And saw with his own eyes all He did far and wide.

He wrote this book to convince all the other Jews
That Jesus was their Messiah who brought them good news.

uction

Jesus told them how they could be forgiven of their sins
And be restored to fellowship with God again.

Matthew shows the fulfillment of Christ and prophecy,
As he quotes the Old Testament quite liberally.

He traces all the generations back to Abraham's time
To prove Jesus comes directly through a kingly line.

This was important information for the people of that day,
Because to the Jewish people their lineage had sway.

He goes on to tell of Jesus' earthly ministry
And the kingdom of God He opened to you and me.

So settle right down and let's begin the true story
About the Messiah who lived and died then ascended into glory.

This is a true account
of Jesus Christ the King,
The Messiah of the Jews
and the message He came to bring.

Matthew traces the generations back to their father Abraham
To show his Jewish readers the thread of God's eternal plan.

Now the actual birth of Jesus happened just like this:
Mary and Joseph were headed toward wedded bliss.

But before the wedding, young Mary sweet and mild
Had a visit from an angel who announced she'd be with child!

Mary responded, "But how can that be?
I'm not yet married and still a virgin, you see."

The angel said, "You've found favor; don't be filled with dread."
Mary responded in faith, "May it be as you've said."

(That part of the story is told in the book of Luke,
But it must be mentioned here so you'll know the rest is no fluke.)

Luke 1:26-38; Matthew 1:1-17

6

600 BC

300 BC

1 BC

JOTHAM
AHAZ
HEZEKIAH
MANASSEH
AMON
JOSIAH
JECONIAH
SHEALTIEL
ZERUBBABEL
ABIHUD
ELIAKIM
AZOR
ZADOK
ACHIM
ELIUD
ELEAZAR
MATTHAN
JACOB
JOSEPH
JESUS 7

PRAYER MAIL

Now poor ol' Joseph
   didn't have a clue,
And when he heard she was pregnant
   wasn't sure what to do.

He loved Mary greatly
   and was a righteous man,
So when he saw the situation
   he came up with a plan.

He would put her away quietly
   and avoid a big scene,
But an angel of the Lord
   came to him in a dream.

He said, "Joseph, son of David,
   do not be afraid.
Take Mary as your wife;
   her child is Holy Spirit made.

"Call the baby 'Jesus'
   for He'll save people from their sin."
So Joseph gladly obeyed
   what the angel spoke to him.

Matthew 1:19-25

8

About this time in the eastern skies,
A star shone so brightly it caught some men's eyes.

They were wise men from a far and distant land,
Who'd heard reports that a new King's birth was at hand.

They followed the star 'til it stopped above them,
And found they'd traveled to the town of Bethlehem.

They each brought a gift
    to the newborn King:
One was frankincense,
    an incense of thanksgiving.

The second was myrrh,
    a perfume used for the dead,
The third was gold, symbolizing
    the crown for His head.

Just think about this, kids,
    for the first time in eternity
Jesus left His home in heaven
    and entered human history!

He took on human flesh
    and came to live as a man
To offer redemption and forgiveness
    straight from God's hand.

Matthew 2:1-11

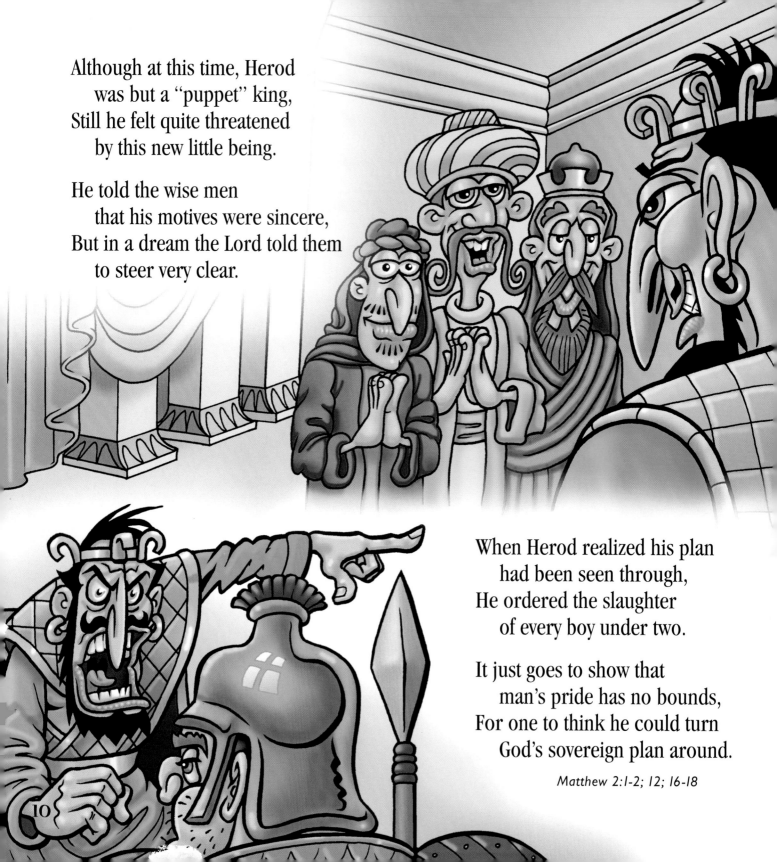

Although at this time, Herod
    was but a "puppet" king,
Still he felt quite threatened
    by this new little being.

He told the wise men
    that his motives were sincere,
But in a dream the Lord told them
    to steer very clear.

When Herod realized his plan
    had been seen through,
He ordered the slaughter
    of every boy under two.

It just goes to show that
    man's pride has no bounds,
For one to think he could turn
    God's sovereign plan around.

Matthew 2:1-2; 12; 16-18

10

So because of the actions of one evil, selfish man,
God spoke again to Joseph and said, "You must leave the land.

"Take the boy to Egypt where you won't live in fear,
And don't return until I tell you that everything's clear."

This fulfilled the prophecies made many years before
That He'd go from Bethlehem to Egypt, then to Galilee's shore.

There are hundreds of prophecies written about Him,
From before He was born until He returns once again.

For God Himself had proclaimed all that would be done
To take His Son to the cross for the sake of His kingdom.

Matthew 2:13-15

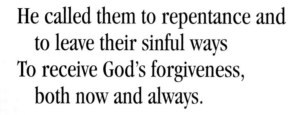

Matthew picks up the story when Jesus is thirty years old.
(About His childhood not very much is told.)

Right about this time Jesus' cousin named John
Told the Jewish people they had to turn from doing wrong.

He called them to repentance and
to leave their sinful ways
To receive God's forgiveness,
both now and always.

You see the Jews at this time
thought they were secured,
That through their history and heritage
their salvation was assured.

But John came and paved the way
for Jesus to replace
The religious rituals of men
with God's precious grace.

Salvation can't be earned by what fallen men will do;
Only mercy and grace are able to see us through.

Before Jesus began His ministry, He asked reluctant John
To baptize Him in water, a rite we still carry on.

John finally agreed and baptized God's perfect One.
Then the heavens opened up, and God acknowledged Him as Son.

Now wouldn't you know, just as things looked their best,
Jesus was led into the desert and given quite a test.

Matthew 3:1-17

He hadn't eaten anything for forty days in all;
He was praying to His Father but Satan wanted Him to fall.

The devil came to Him, and it should come as no surprise
That his goal was to get the Son of God to compromise.

He wanted Jesus to bow down and worship him;
To let go of His trust in God and allow him to win.

You and I face things that are also quite a test.
And the devil knows just where to attack each of us best.

He showed the Lord earthly kingdoms
    and an easier way,
But by the power of the Spirit,
    Jesus never went astray.

Jesus answered him with Scripture
    'cause it's a living sword,
And the devil couldn't stand it
    so he finally left the Lord.

What He did to resist temptation
    God wants us to see,
Is the same escape from sin
    that works for you and for me.

Wash yourself in His Word
    and let it work deep within;
It will strengthen your spirit
    and help you overcome sin.

Matthew 4:1-11

14

We continue with the story
    where we left off before,
As Jesus gathered His disciples
    from Galilee's shore.

He said, "Follow me and
    I'll make you fishers of men!"
So they dropped their nets
    and began to follow Him.

This is still happening
    even to this day,
When people hear the truth
    and decide to obey.

Matthew 4:18-22

Now about this time,
    people began to hear
Of this man named Jesus
    and came from far and near.

He sat them on a mountain
    and began to explain
The paradox of heaven
    and its chief goal and aim.

In this most famous talk called
    "The Sermon on the Mount,"
He tells us how to live
    and make every action count.

Matthew 5-7   **15**

He explained all the ways
   to be happy and blessed.
But I promise you this: it's not
   what you'd have guessed!

He came to proclaim
   His kingdom was at hand,
And tell us how it works
   in ways we'd understand.

Because the thing that
   brings happiness ultimately,
Is to live by God's rules
   'cause they always set us free.

It starts within
   when we submit to God's way,
Then shows up in our actions
   every single day.

There's a part we've come to call
   the Beatitudes
That illustrates for us what
   a life of love includes.

There won't be room for those
   loving power and might
But only for the poor in spirit
   who need Him to live right.

The hard times in life
   allow us to take a firm stand,
And let God demonstrate His power
   showing He's in command.

Matthew 5:3-12

You are most blessed when
    you're at the end of your rope,
'Cause it gives you the chance
    to allow God to be your hope.

It all seems backwards,
    and that's the mystery,
But it's when we die to self
    that we are truly set free.

If we try to own our lives,
    we'll lose them for sure;
But if we submit ourselves to Him,
    we'll be eternally secure.

He said, "Those who love Me
    are like salt and light.
Now take the gospel to a world
    caught in sin's blight.

"Forgive one another
    as God's forgiven you."
And for every human being,
    this *is* the good news!

"I didn't abolish the law,
    but now you walk in grace,
Don't be like the Pharisees,
    who show a false face.

Matthew 5:13-20

17

"Try not to divorce
    but remain forever true;
Be as faithful to your spouse
    as God has been to you.

"Let your yes be yes,
    and your no be no.
If someone asks for your shirt,
    give your coat also.

"Love your enemies and
    for them sincerely do pray,
For even the ungodly cherish
    those who love them everyday.

"Don't act like hypocrites
    who want everyone to know
All they pray and do and give
    'cause it's only for show.

"When you pray, go quietly
    to your Father above.
Give your money in secret,
    and let your life show love.

"Worship God alone
    and seek His ways above all.
He'll never leave your side
    and will answer when you call."

18   *Matthew 5:31-37*

He gave them a guide
   to show how they should pray,
And the lesson hasn't changed
   even to this day.

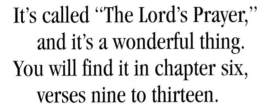

It's called "The Lord's Prayer,"
   and it's a wonderful thing.
You will find it in chapter six,
   verses nine to thirteen.

He spoke other lessons
   of how to best live on earth,
And how to be sure
   you've had a spiritual rebirth.

"Lay up your treasures in heaven
   where they can't be destroyed,
And when you face the Creator,
   you'll be overjoyed!

"Not one of you can add
   a single moment to your life.
You must walk with God daily
   and not give in to strife.

"Do not judge others,
   or you'll be judged too;
By the standard you measure,
   it will be measured to you.

"Ask, seek, and knock,
   and it shall be opened, it's true.
Do unto others
   as you'd have them do to you.

"Beware of false prophets
   who desire to deceive;
You'll know them by their fruit
   and what they believe.

"He who hears these words of Mine
   and acts on them,
Will be as salt and light
   to the world they live in."

He told how to be a citizen
   in His righteous kingdom;
Both here on earth now,
   and in the glorious one to come.

He showed how to be expressions
   of their Father above,
And demonstrated for them
   what it really means to love.

When Jesus finished teaching,
   the people were in awe.
They'd never known such wisdom
   as they now heard and saw.

Matthew 6:9-13; 19-21, 27-34; 7:1-12, 28-29   **19**

Jesus healed every person who had come to Him;
He was filled with compassion as He ministered to them.

There was the leper, the blind men, and the one who was possessed;
The woman who was bleeding, and those who were oppressed.

Once He went to a young girl who had died that day;
He said she was sleeping and sent everyone away.

The people laughed at His words,
 for they knew she was dead.
But Jesus spoke to her,
 and she rose up from her bed.

He said, "Awake My child,
 for you are now well!"
It was one of many miracles
 that people would tell.

He did all these wonders
 in the sight of fallen men,
As proof He was Messiah
 with power to forgive sin.

Matthew 8:1-17; 9:18-26

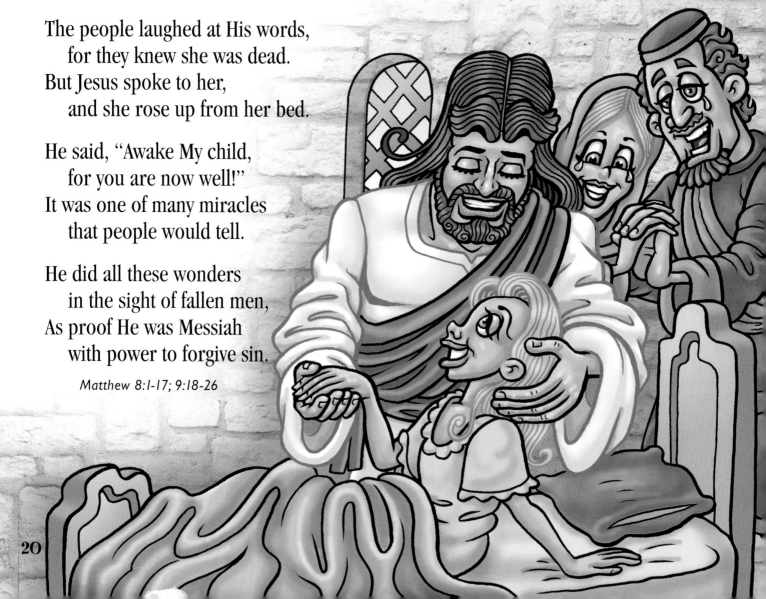

He chose twelve disciples, and these were their names:
Peter, Andrew, John, Philip, Thomas and James,

Simon, Thaddaeus, another James, and Bartholomew,
Judas who betrayed Him, and of course, Matthew.

He gathered His disciples and gave them all authority
To proclaim God's forgiveness and see people set free.

They were to do the same things they'd seen Him do:
Heal the sick, raise the dead, and cleanse the lepers too.

Matthew 10:1-40

21

There was another group of people
    who followed Him,
But their intent was to trap Him
    and do Him in.

They were the Pharisees and Sadducees,
    the religious Jews.
Who hated Jesus and thought
    that He was bad news.

They were sticklers for the law
    and all their traditions;
And He threatened their comfort,
    their power, and positions.

The religious leaders despised Him
    and all He was about.
They were afraid He'd expose them,
    and they'd lose all their clout.

So they put their heads together
    and came up with a plan,
To get rid of God's own Son,
    whom they saw as just a man.

They kept trying to find ways to say He broke their laws.
What they couldn't understand was that He had a higher cause.

If the scene weren't so tragic, you could have a little snort,
That they wanted to put *God* on trial in their religious court!

Matthew 12:1-14; 22-37

When the common folks would gather,
    Jesus would begin
To speak to them in parables,
    while the twelve listened in.

There's the parable of the sower,
    the tares and the wheat,
The hidden treasure, the leaven,
    and the mustard seed.

They were stories He told
    to help the people understand
The mystery He was revealing,
    which was the kingdom at hand.

One day as He was teaching
    it had gotten kinda late,
So He blessed some loaves and fishes
    and somehow everybody ate.

There were five thousand men,
    plus women and children too,
And twelve baskets full of scraps,
    when everyone was through.

The disciples got into a boat
    after He sent the crowd away,
Then went off by Himself
    to a mountain to pray.

Matthew 13:3-52; 14:13-23

He showed up later, walking on the sea.
The disciples were frightened 'til He said, "It's only Me!"

Then Peter cried out, "Lord if it really is You,
Command me to walk out on the water too."

Matthew 14:25-28

The Lord bid him come but when he started to doubt,
He began to sink until the Lord pulled him out.

Jesus said to Peter, "If you'd only believe,
There's no end to what you and I can achieve."

Matthew 14:29-33

25

Jesus asked His men one day,
    "Who do people say I am?"
"John the Baptist or Jeremiah,"
    they answered Him.

"Well, who do *you* say I am?"
    He asked His little squad.
Peter answered, "The Christ,
    the Son of the Living God!" *Matthew 16:13-17*

Then Jesus took with Him
    Peter, James, and John,
And climbed the mountain
    He was transfigured upon.

His clothes became bright;
    His face shone like the sun;
And the voice of God said,
    This is My beloved Son!"

Then Moses and Elijah
    appeared there as well,
And when the three saw this,
    to the ground they fell.

As they left the mountain,
    Jesus tried to explain
The events that lay before Him—
    all the agony and pain.

He was preparing these men for a future day
So they could continue the work after He'd gone away.

26

Matthew 17:1-9

A rich young ruler approached Jesus one day
And said, "I've done everything the law has to say.

"What else must I do for eternal life to impart?"
But Jesus looked at him and saw through to his heart.

He said, "Sell everything and come and follow Me!"
The man turned away sad, for he was quite wealthy.

It's not enough to keep the rules and try to be good;
We must invite Him into our lives so we can live as we should.

At this Peter chimed in and asked, "What awaits me?"
Jesus said, "You'll sit on a throne and rule eternally."

Matthew 19:16-22

He told them of a vineyard and the workers who were hired.
Some were hired right away, then later more were acquired.

At the end of the day each was paid the same wage.
He said, "That's how it will be at the end of the age."

James and John came to Him
    to settle a fight;
One wanted to sit on His left
    and one on His right.

The other ten were angry
    and began to get irate,
But Jesus challenged them asking,
    "You want to be great?

"Well, the greatest in My kingdom
    is the one who serves,
And when it's all said and done,
    he'll get what he deserves."

He went on to tell them
    of His death and resurrection;
He wanted them to understand
    that this was God's direction.

Matthew 20:1-17; 20-27

Jesus told two disciples
to find a donkey for Him
For His triumphant ride
into Jerusalem.

All the Jews were gathering
for the Passover feast
That they all celebrated
from the oldest to the least.

When the crowds saw the donkey with its precious load,
They cut palm branches and laid them down on the road.

"Hosanna!" they cried. "Blessed is He who has come
In the name of the Lord" as He entered Jerusalem.

Matthew 21:1-11

29

When the chief priests and scribes
   heard the crowds clap,
They questioned His authority
   and tried to set a trap.

"Should we pay a tax or not?"
   they asked with sly nods.
He said, "Give to Caesar what is his,
   and to God what is God's."

He called them all hypocrites
   and was filled with disgust.
He saw their wicked hearts
   and where they put their trust.

Matthew 22:15-22

He called out their sins
   and the bondages they kept,
And when He looked out
   over Jerusalem, Jesus wept.

Matthew 22:23-39

Jesus walked out of the temple
and began to prophesy
About the end of the age and
a day when people would cry.

"There will be wars and famine
and earthquakes too,
False prophets will come
to try and mislead you.

"But the Gospel will be preached
to every nation
And then comes the 'abomination
of desolation.'

"For there is coming
a great tribulation,
Such has not been seen
in all of creation.

"The sun will be darkened
and the stars will fall;
The heavens will be shaken,
then you'll hear the judgment call.

"When this will take place
has not been shown;
That knowledge is reserved
for the Father alone."

Matthew 24:1-31

He told of ten virgins—five foolish and five wise—
Who waited past midnight for the bridegroom to arrive.

The five with plenty of oil entered the banquet hall,
But the five who had none missed the bridegroom's call.

To those who are faithful more will be given;
To the ones who are not, everything will be taken.

When the Son of Man returns, He'll sit on His glorious throne.
He'll separate all the goats from the sheep who are His own. *Matthew 25:1-13*

When Jesus had finished explaining everything
He went with Simon the leper to spend the evening.

A woman came up and poured out costly perfume.
It ran down His head, and the fragrance filled the room.

His disciples saw the scene and began to react,
But Jesus told everyone it was a beautiful act.

Her simple gesture was a sign to everyone
Of the burial that awaited God's only Son.

Matthew 26:6-13   **33**

During the Passover Feast
of unleavened bread,
Jesus ate with His disciples
and this is what He said:

"Take and eat My body,
    which is broken for you."
Then handed them a cup saying,
    "Drink from this too.

"This symbolizes the blood
    of a new covenant,
That will bring forgiveness of sin
    when people repent."

Matthew 26:26-28

He said sadly,
    "One of you will betray
The Son of Man
    on this very day."

Judas Iscariot
    left to meet with the Chief Priest
To be paid for his betrayal
    and didn't care in the least.

Matthew 26:14-16; 20-22

34

Jesus warned His disciples
   they would all fall away,
But Peter protested,
   "You I never would betray!"

Jesus looked at him with love
   as One who knows,
And said, "You'll deny Me three times
   before the cock crows."

Matthew 26:31-35

35

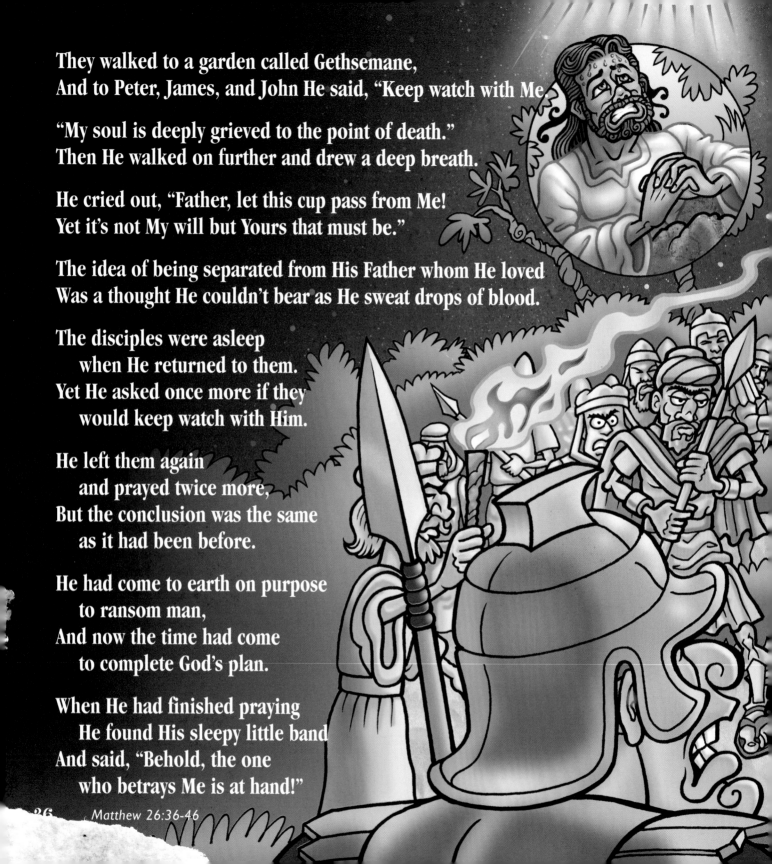

They walked to a garden called Gethsemane,
And to Peter, James, and John He said, "Keep watch with Me.

"My soul is deeply grieved to the point of death."
Then He walked on further and drew a deep breath.

He cried out, "Father, let this cup pass from Me!
Yet it's not My will but Yours that must be."

The idea of being separated from His Father whom He loved
Was a thought He couldn't bear as He sweat drops of blood.

The disciples were asleep
   when He returned to them.
Yet He asked once more if they
   would keep watch with Him.

He left them again
   and prayed twice more,
But the conclusion was the same
   as it had been before.

He had come to earth on purpose
   to ransom man,
And now the time had come
   to complete God's plan.

When He had finished praying
   He found His sleepy little band
And said, "Behold, the one
   who betrays Me is at hand!"

Matthew 26:36-46

The events of the evening happened like this:
Judas told the priests and elders he'd give Jesus a kiss.

They came for Him with torches and the sword,
And Judas walked up and betrayed the Lord.

An angry mob surrounded Jesus
and closed in from the rear.
Then Peter grabbed a sword
and cut off a guard's ear.

Jesus rebuked him saying,
"It must happen like this!"
Then He healed the man's ear
so nothing was amiss.

Jesus went peacefully
and didn't try to break free;
He'd made the choice to obey
the Father's decree.

He came to lay down His life;
no one took it from Him.
So He had to go along
with the plans of evil men.

"I could call a legion of angels
and they'd come and rescue Me,
But My purpose is to die for you,
and I do so willingly."

Matthew 26:47-54 **37**

Those who seized Him
    took Him off to stand trial,
And during that time
    Peter made his first denial.

The chief priests and council
    found people who would lie
About all He'd said and done
    'cause they wanted Him to die.

In a fit of frustration
    when he should have been awed,
The High Priest cried out,
    "Are You the Son of God?"

"It is as you say," Jesus
    answered in a hushed breath.
"You blaspheme!" the priest cried,
    "You deserve death!"

They beat Him with their hands
    and they spit in His face;
They taunted and tortured
    God's marvelous gift of grace.

Matthew 26:57-68

For the third time Peter said,
   "That Man I do not know!"
Then he turned and saw Jesus
   and heard the cock crow.

When Judas saw what he'd done,
   he was filled with remorse;
But it was much too late
   to change his awful course.

While Peter went out
   and wept bitterly,
Judas hanged himself
   from the branch of a tree.

Matthew 26:69-75; 27:3-5

Jesus went before Pilate, the governor of Rome,
Who said, "This man is innocent, let Him go home."

It was a tradition at this time that during the Feast
The people could ask to have a prisoner released.

Matthew 27:11-15

40

"Give us Barabbas," the frenzied crowd cried,
"And let that man Jesus be CRUCIFIED!"

They took a crown of thorns and smashed it on His head;
They mocked Him and beat Him, but not a word He said.

Matthew 27:20-23; 29

41

**T**hey stripped Him of His clothes,
His robe, and His shoes,
They jeered and made a sign that read,
"THE KING OF THE JEWS."

They marched Him up a hill
and nailed Him to a tree,
And on that unforgettable day,
Christ died for you and me.

They hung Him on a cross
between two who were thieves.
Then drove nails through His hands
and both of His feet.

At that very moment
He bore all the world's sin,
And the face of God the Father
turned away from Him.

He cried out, "My God,
why hast Thou forsaken Me?"
As the Son was separated
from the Trinity.

Jesus cried out once more
saying, "It is finished!"
And the perfect Lamb of God
died sin-blemished.

Matthew 27:27, 37-46, 50

They pierced His side
  with the thrust of a sword;
He was counted as a criminal,
  this Man who was the Lord.

When He died the temple veil
  was torn in two,
The earth shook so violently
  that the rocks split too.

God shed His own blood
  on the hill of Calvary,
To free us from sin's power
  and its awful penalty.

He bore every sin of each man,
  woman, and child
That through His death and resurrection
  we could be reconciled.

He defeated death
  and took Hades' key;
He paved the way of redemption
  for you and me.

At that very moment
  time was forever split in two;
It became "before and after"
  for both me and you.

Matthew 27:51-52

43

Meanwhile to everyone who loved Him
    things looked bleak.
They didn't understand
    what would happen that week.

They took Jesus' body
    and laid it in a tomb,
And all of His followers
    were filled with gloom.

But the best part of the story
    is that it's not yet done.
Listen very carefully
    'cause the best is yet to come!

Guards were placed at the tomb
    to keep watch and see
That His body wasn't stolen
    in a vast conspiracy.

Matthew 27:62-66

44

But on the third day when
   the women went to the grave,
They saw to their surprise
   that the stone was rolled away.

An angel of the Lord
   spoke and said to them,
"Don't be afraid,
   I know you're looking for Him.

"He is not here I tell you,
   He arose just as He said.
Go tell His disciples
   Jesus has risen from the dead!"

They ran with fear and joy
   to shout their news:
"Jesus is alive! He's
   the true Messiah of the Jews!"

Matthew 28:1-8

45

Jesus arose triumphant
  and sits at God's right hand
And He'll return again
  at the Father's command.

Since that Easter morning,
  nothing's been the same!
It's for this very reason
  that to the earth He came.

Then Jesus went and spoke
  to the remaining eleven.
He said, "All authority is Mine
  on earth and in heaven.

"Go now and make followers
  of every nation."
That is what is known
  as the Great Commission.

Matthew 28:19-20

47

Let's come and bow before Him
with a grateful heart,
And decide at this very moment
to let Him give us a fresh start.

Let us live our lives
following our loving Lord,
Making disciples of all nations,
and living in one accord.

Ask Him to help you tell others
of God's good news,
And help them understand
so they can follow Him too!